SINK THE BELGRANO!
with
MASSAGE

By the same author

WEST and other plays

KVETCH and ACAPULCO

THE TRIAL and METAMORPHOSIS (Amber Lane Press)

EAST: AGAMEMNON AND THE FALL
OF THE HOUSE OF USHER (John Calder)

DECADENCE and GREEK (John Calder)

GROSS INTRUSION AND OTHER STORIES (John Calder)

SINK THE BELGRANO!
WITH
MASSAGE

STEVEN BERKOFF

faber and faber
LONDON · BOSTON

First published in 1987 by
Faber and Faber Limited
3 Queen Square London WC1N 3AU

Photoset and printed in Great Britain by
Redwood Burn Limited Trowbridge Wiltshire

British Library Cataloguing in Publication Data

Berkoff, Steven
Sink the Belgrano! and Massage.
I. Title II. Berkoff, Steven. Massage
822'.914   PR6052.E588

ISBN 0–571–14717–8

SINK THE BELGRANO!

CHARACTERS

MAGGOT SCRATCHER
PIMP
NIT
CHORUS
COMMAND
TELL
WOODY
TOMMY
PRESIDENT OF ARGENTINA
FEET
SIR FISH FACE
REASON
SAILORS
FARMERS

For Clara

Sink the Belgrano! was first performed at the Half Moon Theatre on 2 September 1986. The cast was as follows:

MAGGOT SCRATCHER	Maggie Steed
PIMP	Barry Stanton
NIT	Bill Stewart
CHORUS	Rory Edwards
COMMAND	Terence McGinty

Other parts were played by Tom Dean Burn, George Dillon, Eugene Lipinski and Edward Tudor Pole

Director	Steven Berkoff
Designer	Ellen Cairns
Music	Mark Glentworth

This production of *Sink the Belgrano!* subsequently transferred to the Mermaid Theatre, when MAGGOT SCRATCHER was played by Louise Gold.

THE SET

The stage was divided into three areas. Upstage, on a rostrum running left and right, was the political area with desk, and behind it a large screen for projecting images. Downstage, on the main playing area, was drawn the outline of a huge submarine. The actors playing chorus and submariners would do their 'work-outs' and acting from this area. Stage left was a pub area which represented the 'voice of England'. Here the sailors would recline as the people back home and relate to the news as it came in. There was just a round table in the pub area and a dartboard facing off stage. Music accompanied the action, marked entrances and exits, and created a very strong atmosphere under the deft handling of Mark Glentworth. The actors played all the roles from Falkland farmers to Members of Parliament and, of course, the main roles as young, physically fit submariners. Props were kept to a minimum and were largely a change of hat or a red and white football scarf. The sailors wore track suits throughout which was a simple neutral uniform. The chorus were dressed in plain suits. I have not indicated the kind of slides I used since this would be a personal choice, but I have indicated where it might be necessary to project the text on to the screen.

S.B.

THE STILL SMALL VOICE OF TRUTH

CHRONICLE OF INCONSISTENCIES

On Tuesday 4 May, 1982, the House of Commons heard a statement from the then Secretary of State for Defence, John Nott. People, Press and Parliament were given to understand that the forty-four-year-old USS Phoenix, survivor of Pearl Harbour, for such the Belgrano was, had to be sunk by our nuclear submarine, because she was converging on the Task Force. Albeit there had until that moment been no British casualties in action, I and others did not criticize. Daily from 2 April, we had publicly opposed the sending of the Task Force, and urged its return, but we recognized that terrible things happen, once conflict starts. No Belgrano – No Sheffield, No Ardent, No Antelope, No Atlantic Conveyor, No Coventry, No Bluff Cove, No Goose Green. But Mrs Thatcher would have been deprived of the Military Victory, which was what, for her, the Falklands War was all about.

I began to ask questions about the Belgrano in July 1982, when HMS Conqueror returned to the West Coast of Scotland. The Captain, Commander Christopher Wreford-Brown, DSO, made it clear that he had sunk the Belgrano, not on the impulse of defending the Task Force, but 'on orders from Northwood'. This was very different from the impression given to Parliament, Press, and People. Small inconsistencies tend to be part of larger inconsistencies – small lies part of larger lies. For example, it was dragged out of Ministers that Belgrano had been detected not on 2 May at 8p.m., but on 30 April at 4p.m. A series of Parliamentary Questions and Debates, the Old Bailey Trial of Clive Ponting, the Minority Report of the Foreign Affairs Select Committee published in July 1985, add up to a picture of a Prime Minister, aware of the Peruvian Peace Proposals, ordering the sinking of the Belgrano, at Chequers, on 2 May, not for reasons of military necessity but for reasons of political advantage.

Tam Dalyell MP, July, 1986

It had to be written. What a story! All those statements and contra-
dictions in the House of Commons. All those 'statesmen' lying
their little heads off in the Commons, and then when the facts
emerged having to contradict themselves. What a pack of fakes,
and what a disgusting bunch of rogues. It is apparent to everyone
that the sinking of the *Belgrano* was a very dubious affair and led to
the severe attacks on the British Fleet and subsequent huge loss of
life. How many people realize that before that calculated piece of
sabotage not one British soldier had died! After unloosing that torpedo under orders not from the submarine *Conqueror* but from
England on a ship way outside the demilitarized zone all havoc
broke loose. It was a calculated gamble to end the war at a stroke
and failed miserably. My play deals with the situation as I found it
and was inspired by the book by Arthur Gavshon and Desmond
Rice. I met Desmond on New Year's Eve in 1984 and mutually
expressing our disgust on the incident of the *Belgrano* sinking led
him to introduce his book to me. It made a fascinating and sordid
read. I could never understand people who could order the taking
of life so easily and weep later at the havoc they caused. I imagine
such people to be 'armoured' in the full Reichian sense, dead to all
real human response except what concerns them personally. The
lack of imagination to foresee events is typical of right-wing thinking. The pollution of the environment and their lame excuses for
not dealing with it; the deadly poisoning of our seas with nuclear
wastes; acid rain; bursting prisons – all seem to have one common
heritage and that to me is an abnormal disregard for human life and
values. Plus an overwhelming and religious belief in the sanctity of
the marketplace. The *Belgrano* sinking was a typical product of
that muddled and opportunist thinking. The irony is that brave
Britons and Argentinians lost their lives needlessly. The play
received mixed reviews and some virulent ones from the right-
wing press. It was curious that their reviews, which were almost
hysterical cant, resembled so closely the threats and poisoned mail
I received from Fascist thugs. Special thanks to Desmond Rice and

a special thanks to the Half Moon Theatre, and Chris Bond, who took the chance and gave his unstinting support.

S.B.

CHORUS: Oh you most brave and valiant Englishmen
Who never shall, no never bear the yoke
Of shame or curdled pride beneath the boot
Of some o'erweening greasy foreign bloke.
We smashed the damned Spanish might...
We put the Hun upon the British rack,
The Boers we kicked to kingdom come
And now the Argies sneaked behind our back.
Oh blasted glory for a few frail days
Oh cowards hiding under the sheep
Like Ulysses they sneaked while Britain dazed
Worn out with strikes and social strife
Numb with queues of unemployed that add
Their groaning weight to the nation's back...
But once aroused, oh ho! old Albion snorts
The Bulldog, start-eyed, drools for Argy blood
Outraged its precious garden overrun
By foreign, greasy, dark unholy scum.
Oh howl fair noble Grand Bretagn
Your people's voices crying out from afar
Like babies howling for the mother's breast
While dark satanic forces raid its nest
We put the greedy scavenger to flight
With fists of steel and hawk-like Harrier jets
Our submarines like silent hungry sharks
Went hunting for the juicy Argy game
But they were cautious, hiding, wouldn't show
Hoping for a *fait accompli* for their crime
And crawling behind the skirts of the UNO.

PIMP: Oh shit your royal sweetest Maggot,
The lousy Argy swines unleashed their bile
On us, decided to invade our Falkland
Paradise, and dead of night they came like rats

3

Disturbed the peace and placed their rot,
Which means their scummy Argy flag upon our
Holy God-gave Promised Land!

MAGGOT: Those bloody junta bloody swine . . . !
How dare they, how simply do they bloody dare
When we've been so damned good to them
Never complained when their death squads
Got rid of opposition in mass graves . . .
Nor publicly showed our disgust at torture
For those that disobeyed (since naturally we
Wish to trade) and now those greasy Argy wogs
Show their thanks by stealing our sweet
Frecious lands. Call out the Fleet, get planes
And tanks, I love to have a crisis on my hands.

PIMP: We'll get the UNO behind us first
Give evidence and facts to thwart their claim.

MAGGOT: What bloody claim! When gangsters rob
What fuels their greed, you Pimp, is gain.
Don't talk to me of robbers justifying
Deeds, the land is ours, that's plain to see.

PIMP: I know that and you know that but they
May say that we, that is those ghosts of past
Who made up our great history, did steal it,
Pardon the expression, first . . . in 1833 we staked
Our claim, backed by a warship, ma'am, or two
And threw the Argies off the land, and now
Although through time it's ours . . . like some
Adopted babe we suckled, and watched it grow
Like our own flesh, the mother wants it back again.
So let's go to the world's great states
And get them behind us in our claim
The child we reared must then decide
The Islanders' wishes cannot be denied
And naturally all of them will want to stay British.

MAGGOT: No! No! No! That's not the way, not that.
To sit around, regurgitate old tales
Who owned it then and now and chat
Until we grow old, like ancient cronies in a pub

4

Recounting how we owned this piece of sod
Discounting claims and waving old contracts
Possession is you know nine-tenths the law
And he who transgresses our hard-won right
Will get himself one hell of a bloody fight.

PIMP: We must of course recourse to written law
'Tis true that they have stolen our sweet lands
But then there will be time the world will judge
Without perhaps a punch-up strewn in blood
To save lives surely is the way
With honour we will live another day.

MAGGOT: Oh bloody bollacks compromise you mean
And wait in turn for others to redeem our wealth
And sit in calm compliance while we hope
For others to present to us a deal,
While whispering give up old colonial ties
As they in turn make profits with their trade
Their greed to capture markets far and wide
Will sugar every bloody thing they say
And in the end we'll give the bloody lot away!
By the way Pimp ... where is the Falklands??

Falkland Farmers

FARMER 1: Oh toil, oh strife, oh bleeding blooding graft
Is this the life for us I daily spout?
For sixty quid a week they bleed our veins
And us poor farmers slave for next to nought
We live in this pisspot, this dreary rock
Where no one has invested, not a jot ...
The profits never go to thee or me,
Where then? The bloody bleedin' FIC.

FARMER 2: What's that?

FARMER 1: The bloody Falkland Island Company!

FARMER 2: What's that ...?

FARMER 1: Those who pontz from distant lands
Who own more than forty per cent
Of this, this wind-spat spit of rock,

5

And take the wool, our precious locks,
They own our house, they keep us poor
And we buy our grub at the company store.
FARMER 2: So bloody bleedin' bloomin' hell
While we sit on this blasted heath
They chat about our future rights
And say our wishes must be paramount
Bollacks and lockjaw, scum and dregs!
They've done sweet FA all these years
No roads are built, no hospitals . . .
When we are ill or hurt we fly
To Argy land where Argy hands
Repair our broken bodies or we'd die
So all that's cock and bollacks when they say
We fight for you dear folks in case one day
The Argies make you drive the right-hand way.
FARMER 1: It makes good PR back in gutter press
Who suck up lies more quickly than
Do buzzing flies the garbage in a bin.
They leave behind their maggot worms
That crawl across their daily sheets,
You think the Government has a heart
In thinking of the welfare of us men?
When really their souls couldn't give a fart.
Oh bullshite soggy Scratcher spews
Her eyes are on some distant parts
Antarctica or oil, that makes a start . . .
PIMP: How dare you pigs complain, you dogs
You curs that *want* always and gripe
Then know we care for you like we
Might care for chickens in our pens
You've never had it quite so good
Regular employment, lots of space
And all you do is trim some wool
And drink yourselves into an early grave
Of course we can't worry for you.
Eighteen hundred poor souls that sweat
And piss their lives away in hell

More than that number's killed themselves
Died by their own hand from dire grief
Of unemployment while millions weep.
The nation's fit and young queue up
In grey drab cities where empty days
Will lead to pointless nights, 'Time please'
And at the end your dole queue pay.

MAGGOT: So you think how lucky you are here
You might be back in England's drear
And pleasant land where miners strike
And other left-wing pests unite
Like filthy dogs disturb our rest...
Now shuffle off and do some work
While we take on the nation's pain
You're useless, any excuse to shirk,
You're lucky to have me, so don't complain...

NIT: (Rushing on) Oh, your precious whitened hairs
Though now so stained with Sassoon's dyes
Would stand on end if now you knew
How Argentina plotted and spied.

MAGGOT: Stop spitting in my tea, you nit,
Inform me where and when this came
Catastrophe, who can we blame!!
The Labour Party, they failed, you tit.
Wake up, you git, we need a war...
Establish once again our might and strength
Shake our old mane, out fly the moths
Oh God, I start to feel myself again
Now where is this damn Falkland Isle?

NIT: 'Tis just a tiny spot of land
That sits so neat in threshing seas
Not far but far enough 'tis nearer
To the Argentines than us I fear.
Some eight thousand sea miles from Cornwall's toe
And stands four hundred miles from Argy shores
Which thus have tempted them to claim
The Malvinas are theirs once again.

MAGGOT: Again! Again! They never were, you mug.

7

They're British damn you sink that in your bontz.
Again! Just 'cause they leapt across the straits
While we were napping, dealing with the world
They sought to steal our gateway to the south
That precious stepping stone that we may need
Since raging conflict 'twixt the super states
May give a base to our dear USA.
Suppose the Commie swine made use of it
Oiling the Argy hand with swingeing bribe
Eh? What then? Tell me that, you silly prat.

NIT: A dame of iron, for that is what you are,
They never will question your metal now.
Bring forth men soldiers only for thy
Undaunted metal should compose nothing but wars.

CHORUS: And so the valiant British soldiered on
Girded their loins with Vulcan steel
The forge breathed fire night and day
Preparing ships stacked full of cannon shells
Like giant whales of death they steamed ahead
The Harriers like mosquito's wings
Did leap up in the sky were thirty-two
Next stomach loaded full like gorged beasts
Dread bombers, sixteen Victors tore the air
Armed to the teeth with missiled brains
To smell the Argy fear and chase
Locked on to their frightened fleeing game
Next, Scimitar and Scorpion tanks
As deadly as their name suggests,
Mine-sweepers . . . laser-guided bombs
Four hundred thousand tons of fuel
One hundred thousand tons of freight
To concentrate our Scratcher's boys
Into one deadly fist of hate.
We made a bridge across the seas
Which measured some eight thousand miles
And poured twenty-eight thousand noble men
To gain back our sweet Falkland Isles . . .

Inside the submarine *Conqueror*

TOMMY: All right we've heard the news let's get stuck in,
    And sail our deadly turd-shaped tube
    That will unleash pure havoc when
    Upon the surface of the deep we spy
    Some vessel filled with Argentines
    And shit some pain as it glides by
    With hunter-killer submarines
    Deep down we'll dive into the ocean's guts
    And wait . . . just still and silent till
    At last we see that great fat ship
    And then at last we'll have our . . .
CREW: (Sing) 'Sweet violets . . .'
SAILOR 1: Here, hang about and just a mo'
    Before we get all bleedin' hot
    Now sod all this, don't swallow shit
    Don't gulp down all you hear you fool
    You ape, you asshole that is used
    By others who make up the rules
    'You're just a soldier now, go kill'
    'Go Fido, fetch' Don't think mate, no,
    Don't use no skill . . .
    Just obey orders that's your job
    Become a murderer's right hand . . .
    Don't dare to question what we do
    For what we are protecting and for who!
SAILOR 2: Protecting life and limb and British soil
    Sod you, who do you think made war?
    Who stepped upon the British corn?
    Who, mate, bloody started this all?
    For self-determination of the Falkland folk
    To make an omelette you gotta break some yolks.
SAILOR 1: What's self-determination mate?
    Do you know what the fuck it means?
    You just shove big words down your throat
    Like when mum gave you medicine . . .
    Now open up and down it goes, good boy.

Whenever hard truth won't go down
We grease the way with subtle quotes,
Self-determination, paramount, law and order,
All that crap. Old Adolf smashed Slovakia
To protect his German hordes
Sudetenland must have, he said,
Self-determination for those Nazi bores.

SAILOR 3: Then fuck off off this boat you cunt
Don't fucking winge, you got no guts
A soldier's life's obey the Queen
The thinking's done by Whitehall nuts
We know there's right and wrong on both
But basically we trust our state
You must believe in England's green
And pleasant or fucking emigrate.

SAILOR 1: I'll fight . . . I'll hold a gun . . . I'll kill
I'll support the Union Jack, so help me I will
But I'll not stuff a sock in it
I'll not become a sponge for all
Just use your brains and think at last
Before it's blown away because
You kept your brainbox up your ass.

COMMAND: Now, now, lads, let's cool it down, eh?
The bloody war's not our responsibility
Now is it? Bloody hell . . . just think
If we had to unscramble every wrong,
Undo the twisted knot of history each time
We sink a foreign ship with our sweet bombs
We'd spend our time in Davy Jones'
Deep down still gassing, who did wrong?
Or else blown up upon the choppy green
Discussing politics as we cling
To shattered mast heads in the freezing sea.
No, boys, you volunteered, you came aboard
Because you like the adverts on TV
You want to be a hero, fire a gun . . .
Wear fancy helmets in your jets
As you ascend into the sky like Zeus

Like a god, omnipotent, a silver bird.
With nuclear claws you tear and kill
Or else beneath the deep as deadly sharks
Your finger on the button, death all round
You deal your piercing strike and wait
Until the bomb slips silently, no sound
Is made until it swiftly penetrates
Like a hot knife into butter . . .
It sinks into the bowels of the ship
Into steel plate it cuts and rips
And from the wounds issue its life
Machines and oil, smoke and blood
And then the sea replaces all that space
And claims the ship like carrion back again
That's why you're here, yes, that's your job!

SAILOR I: I see, we're just a bunch of yobs.

COMMAND: That's right, you've got it, boy,
Don't look for principles in politics
It's just a game they play, you're Whitehall's toys
You're here to kill or die, not reason bloody why
Did we go in 'gainst bloody Ian Smith
When he seized power in '65? . . . No Task Force
Then rushed in and said we're here to defend
Rhodesia's black men . . .
And do not think for old Hong Kong
We'll go in there and fight, no fear,
China's a bit too big for us my dear.

SAILOR I: So it's all a question of size or race?

COMMAND: You've got it sonny in this case
You're the Task Force boys . . . we rule the waves
'Cause if you don't, you'd better pray.

Cabinet

MAGGOT: Where's my Foreign Secretary Pimp
And get me my good faithful Nit
Those two defenders of Tory strength.

PIMP and NIT: Here your worshipful most honoured Maggot.

MAGGOT: Well, what's the news today my boys?
Come on Pimp don't slobber and winge,
If the news is bad just spit it out
I've not all day to see you cringe
I must get Denis's supper soon,
And if you don't unheave your load
I'll not get the best sides of bacon home
So don't annoy me with your stutter
Just open your cake-hole and sodding utter.

PIMP: It's good and bad oh holy Scratcher.

MAGGOT: (Aside) *I loathe these fair and foul male turds*
Still, I'll throw them out but screw them first.

PIMP: They want to make with us peace terms.

MAGGOT: They bloody what? Why peace terms now?
After they shit on our front door.

PIMP: It seems (well not exactly our front door
More like the garden gate or tradesman's
Entrance so to speak) . . .
It seems that having made their little *coup*
Or *fait accompli* . . . it's up to you.
They're willing now to sue for peace, i.e.
A recognition of their claims . . .
Historic rights when Spain left Argentina
How Malvinas are to them their symbol
Of the time when they kicked Spain
Right up the ass and now they want
To introduce the boot to us . . .

NIT: We seized the place in 1833 and now
It's been so long it really does belong
To us . . . it's practice . . . it's ours . . .
For a century or more our folk
Have toiled the soil and reared their young.

MAGGOT: Oh shut up, Nit, you'll make me weep
And anyhow who asked you to speak
Just shut your trap, you're M.o.D.
That means defence if you can't read.
I have a well-paid politician here
Called Pimp who interprets history

12

Or bends it here and there if there
Be need . . . What say you, Pimp, the world's with us?
Have you checked old Cowboy yet,
Old Geriatric Joe, is he for us?

PIMP: Without a doubt, he's for us like you
Can't believe . . . sends all his love
And will give all the info that we need.
Like how much weaponry they've got and where
How many planes, what ships, what subs,
He'll loan his radar, high frequency
To intercept and translate any code
That they may send, just point your
Guns and trust him, he'll do the rest.

MAGGOT: Oh Jolly Joe . . . old Cowboy Poke
Oh what a friend indeed when times
Are tough and then a friend we need
To help us smooth the way . . .
How sweet . . . He said all that? Aah Joe
I must invite the old sod back . . .
His wife's though such an evil bore
Why is it great blokes marry such whores?

BOTH: Hmmmn . . . hmmnnnn . . . hmmmmn . . .?!

MAGGOT: Oh never mind . . . just fuck all that,
Oh shit . . . a pound of bacon with no fat
I'll be back, just chat away . . .
I've got to get the groceries . . .
And please don't quarrel when I've gone
Or plot behind my back!! You scum.

BOTH: My lady . . . would we do that?

PIMP: Oh fuck, oh shit, oh piss, oh balls.

NIT: What's the problem old boy . . . Do let me hear.

PIMP: We just bloody sold to Argentina
Some missiles and some naval weaponry
Two hundred million quids' worth flogged
Which may be used against our Fleet
Oh hot bollacks and spotted dick
Our own weapons may like to find
Their way back to their master's house

Weapons of death carry no names
The more's the problem, who can we blame?

SAILOR 1 : Dear Tina, we've passed the Canary Isle
One periscope-depth run each thirty hours
Just to keep us on our toes
This is beginning to feel like fun.

NIT: Oh Pimp, you pontz, you prat, you cur . . .
You, the Foreign Secretary, that what you are?
Did you not suspect that one day
The bloody Argies would get itchy feet
And aim their guns at the British Fleet!
PIMP: Who was to know? Well not for sure
We sell death weapons to those who
Pay. Who cares who they kill, it's their war,
We only manufacture death, no more.
We don't tell who to shoot and kill
We flog the bloody stuff, that's all . . .
But usually it's not our doorstep
We have deigned to shit upon.
South Africa's too far away . . .
We made a bomb in Lebanon . . .
Excuse me! . . . I mean a killing . . .
Oh no! I mean we made a fortune
Selling death all round the world
Is it my fault that now by chance
A bloody boomerang's been hurled?

SAILOR 2: Dear Janet, we've been going five days
I miss you but it won't be long
I'll take some pics, the blokes are nice
For supper we had ice-cream and rice.

MAGGOT: (Re-entering) Well done . . . I got the last half-
pound . . .
He likes it lean and meaty . . . don't we all.
Bastards were just about to close,
I said now what's all this, you work part-time?

14

The Brits are such a lazy bunch of sods
No wonder there's three million unemployed.
The buggers simply now refuse to work
And then the Labour scum will point at me
It's not our bloody sodden fault
It's dole money the state doles out,
They get for free by queueing up
Just once a week, not so much less
Than they would get in full-time graft.
NIT: Then ma'am, why not get wages up?
And so temptation's not so great
The difference being far too much
Between the dole and a week well paid!
MAGGOT: No!! . . . Get *dole* down, and then you'll see
A scramble for the factories . . .
No skiving now, the whistle blows . . .
All present and correct . . . they know
There's now no safety net, that's what they need
That's monetarism, Nit . . . are you agreed?
NIT: Yes, m'lady, I dare say there's truth in that . . .
PIMP: Too bloody true, what . . . ! Lazy scum!
Can't wait to strike at any turn
Been spoilt, what!, by the Welfare State
When what they desperately need is a swift
Kick up the ass mate.
MAGGOT: That's all very well you know,
But the barometer of fate
Has placed us in the opinion polls
Behind the scummy Socialist crud
Behind old stinking 'Feet' we limp
While you just drag your foot
Old 'Feet' just stumbles on and bleats
Like some old flasher on Hampstead Heath.
PIMP: About this invasion my lady . . .
MAGGOT: Shut up a mo' . . . I'm thinking hard . . .
PIMP: Of course, of course, what action to take?
MAGGOT: No! Whether to fry it in butter or lard!
PIMP: Oh myself, I like my bacon grilled . . .

A few tomatoes sizzling there
Bung in a mushroom or two
And if you've time then just prepare
Two slices of fried bread, that's a treat
Or if you like two scrambled eggs
Quick whipped and fluffy like molten gold
Coffee steaming from fresh ground beans
... That's my definition of ecstasy ...

MAGGOT: You're wasted as Foreign Secretary
Your talent there is hardly used
We need a decent bloody chef
The Commons kitchen's the place for you!
(Aside.) *Ah! I have it ... I have it Nit!*

NIT: Yes, my lady, what have you got?
Have you come up with some inspired plot?

MAGGOT: I'll make a Spanish omelette!
At first I'll crack some Argy eggs
Throw in some tasty British herbs
Well flavoured with strong English earth
Then, round and round the cauldron go
In the poisoned entrails throw
Hate and good old Tory guile
Plots to cover up our sins
Lies and slander to beguile
Then throw massive outrage in,
Synthetic will do just as well.
To make the mixture rise and swell
Then add more than one thousand dead
Tears of children's salty brine
Broken hearts and widows pining
Mothers mourning for their lost boys,
Collect those dewdrops to make the paste
Soldiers' howls as they lay burning,
Throw in the lot and keep it turning
Olé, your Spanish omelette!

PIMP: But who will eat this foul stew?

MAGGOT: The entire British press, you fool!

16

The Conqueror

Rule Britannia, Britannia rules the waves
Britain never never never shall be slaves.
We've spent twelve thousand million quid
On our defence in twelve short months
And now you see money well spent
We'll give a demo of our strength
We've got the class and discipline
The training, thank you at your expense,
Communications are next to none
Weapon locating radar-chum
We're on our way from Scotland's shores
Until we reach the battle zone
We're going fast beneath the deep
On our way to the Argy Fleet
Attracting curious sharks and whales
Who cannot believe this giant fish
That slides armed with its deadly eggs
That will be laid when we will mate
War's just another way to fornicate
We'll fuck their slaggy Argy ships
Action stations, we'll rehearse a hit.

SAILOR 3: Dear Sheila, just cleaning my gun
I tell you it's great . . . it's just fun
We're not going to kill anyone
We're just keeping the Argy on the run.

SAILOR 4: Dear Rita, we crossed the Equator today
It weren't half hot, the guys sunbathed
We'll be there in about a week
We're safe as houses and the roof don't leak.

SAILOR 5: Dear Doreen, I feel so proud my love
To be part of this great Fleet
A hundred and seven ships on the way
And each man will say . . . 'I was there that day.'

SAILOR 6: Dear Mum, I can tell you I'm scared
Don't know what we're facing down here

It's so quiet beneath the surface and still
But each night we can watch a film.

SAILOR 7: Dear Dad, it's getting colder as we close in
The South Atlantic's cold as ice
I can't imagine what it's like
If we had to bloody swim.

SAILOR 8: We're told there's now a TEZ,
Total Exclusion Zone I mean,
If we find enemy ships within
Then we can blow them to smithereens.

SAILOR 9: Dear Judy, I don't want to kill
In fact of war I've had enough
The Zone we're told's two hundred miles
So they'll stay out, unless they're tired of life.

COMMAND: Two-hundred-mile Exclusion Zone
So if the buggers stay outside
All we can do is be like cops
And whack them if they stray across.
Still I'm not sentimental, this is war
The Argies began it, but I've no hate
But I wouldn't half like it if they want to play
I've got a lovely bunch of coconuts . . . called Mark 8.

Argentina v. Britain

PRESIDENT OF ARGENTINA: No, we don't wish to fight no
    more
It's a question of principle that's all
We have to settle this old score . . .
The Malvinas belong to us
It's on our continental shelf
It's part of our long history
You have no contracts sealed and signed
You came in 1833 and stole
What was rightfully our land
We never sold it to you
We never gave it to you
So please give it back thank you

We tried so many times to call
To ask you when and how and why
You put us off, we're foreign scum
You ignore the warning signs
'End colonialism in all its forms'
Resolution 2065 . . .
The United Nations wrote that line
Nineteen hundred and sixty-five
For seventeen more long years we wait
And get nothing . . . nothing at all
You would not even negotiate
What did you do for your Malvinas
Nothing, but bleed it, suck it dry,
We supplied the Islands' needs . . .
You gave nothing, nothing at all,
Oh yes, perhaps a little greed . . .

PIMP: All right, old chap, now settle down
Don't get your knickers in a twist,
History is made by time
And in that case you must believe
The Falkland Islands really mine
Or rather ours, sorry slip of the tongue,
You cannot separate the strands of memory
Who's right, who's wrong . . .
'Prescription' is the word that I would choose
Defined in our good dictionary
As, 'a claim founded upon much use'
We've had our good old British stock
For so many long winter years
Toil the earth and break the rocks,
And backs as well with sweat and tears,
It's just a little piece of England now
So be a good chap and piss off
Or else we'll blow you to kingdom come.
You know we're on the way old boy
So why don't you just scuttle off
And show your boss that we mean biz,
OK? There's a lot of muscle on the way

He'll understand that there's no deal,
Just stay put in Argy land
I know it's tough, inflation's high
Five hundred per cent and going up
Wages are low, your debt is huge,
But ... don't use the Falklands for your subterfuge.

CHORUS: Oh for a brace of Exocet missiles
That would ascend the brightest heaven of invention
The sky would be their stage
Super Etendard jets to fly
Six hundred and eighty miles per hour above the waves
The deadly Exocet once it is launched
Cannot be stopped until it strikes
Since radar with its seeing eyes
Can only read what's in the sky
Below ten feet its eyes are blind
Oh who would know the cunning fiends
Had fixed them to their flying wings
We did not dream nor could not know
The bastards had such weaponry
This flying spear of death is quick
You can't shoot down an Exocet
When hurled above the choppy seas
You don't see it till you are hit!

Cabinet

MAGGOT: Well done, Pimp, the bastards know
What follows as the night the day
If they won't move, those junta creeps,
That Britain won't just watch and pray
And see our Islands given away ...
PIMP: I told the bugger, it's up to him
The message could not be more plain
I spelt it out, withdraw or else
The answer could be a lot of pain.
MAGGOT: You're sure we're quite prepared, my Nit,

No fuck-ups now, no tricky biz
The press has swallowed all that shit
And the country's right behind us too.

PIMP: Yes, my lady, we're nearly there
And your speech yesterday when you compared
Yourself to Churchill was a wiz.
Hitler's very useful in time like this.

MAGGOT: Never mind all that, just give us facts
We must be certain we will win
Not land our boys into the fat
Because you screwed up, you nit.

NIT: We're all prepared, the Yanks are there
We will know when it's time to hit
Old Cowpoke's loaned the electronic toys
We can even hear them take a shit.

MAGGOT: Spare me your squalid anal jokes
Your public schoolboy legacy, Nit!

NIT: Yes ma'am . . . sorreeeeee!

MAGGOT: What about those bloody Exocets
Those rotten greedy French have flogged
The French are not averse to deals that stank
They'll climb down sewers to make a franc.

NIT: It's all arranged, they'll spill the beans
And tell us the secret of those stinging bees
The intimate details, how fast how high
And how easy it will be to swat them from the sky
We have no need to worry ma'am
We know all they can hurl at us
An inventory you might say
The French have been a good ally.

MAGGOT: How long, how long before our arm
Can swat you might say, with our might?

NIT: Three weeks is all we need, three weeks
And then we'll be right there on sight.

MAGGOT: OK, Pimp, here's the plan, unplug your ears
For three weeks then you show restraint
Talk peace, remonstrate the wrongs,
Make amends, negotiate, discuss

The pros and cons, offer a plan . . .
A waiting time before it's time to go,
'Time please' we go out gently from
The pub with easy and all friendly smiles
The landlord must lock up the doors
And so like us he will away
Into the night, we had our day
And quaffed down our pint
Just look after our good folk
Perhaps a golden handshake and Amen.

PIMP: Oh goody then there'll be no war!
Just threaten and then make a deal
A long lease back, divide the oil?
The Islanders can go to hell.

MAGGOT: No, Pimp, you rotten little turnip
You greasy stupid dotty sod . . .
That's what they'll *think* – why divvy up?
When we can have it all . . .
If we let UNO back in,
Sit down for weeks with Garlic Chops
Debate our terms with the gangster mob
We'll look like we've been shat upon.
We're not a third power yet you know
We've got some balls in the old bird yet
Though I doubt the pair of you
Have got much there to boast about
If we decided to talk to them . . .
To negotiate with those we hate?!
Then goodbye Tory Party from the land.
We're two per cent behind the Reds,
That's all we need to show how weak
And spineless we are to old 'Feet'
They'll shit on us from a great height
Can you see Feet in Downing Street?
Because we couldn't make the pace?
Besides I don't intend to move,
I just redecorated the bloody place.

CHORUS: Around the land, in every pub,
In every dining room and lounge
The voice of England can be heard
Discussing the Falklands with angry sounds
As if the family jewels had been thieved.
Outraged. The telly on, the pot of tea
Refuelling parched throats for verbal war
You'd never believe until last week
They didn't know Falklands from Leigh-on-Sea.

The Commons

MAGGOT: We didn't know, no, not a thing.
Bolt from the blue . . . I couldn't believe . . .
There we were eating their meat,
Enjoying west-end musicals inspired by their chiefs,
How does it go? It's really quite sweet
'Don't cry for me, Argentina'
We were shocked, shocked we were . . .
You know it's quite a strain
We weren't prepared, no ships, no planes,
Not a dicky bird was said . . .
If only they had asked us nicely . . .
Said, 'Please Maggot, can we have our Island
Back', polite and quietly,
We would have considered, I would have said,
'Piss off, you greasy fascist pigs'
(Cheers.)
'Go screw your mother, you filthy wogs'
(Cheers.)
'You want to put your dirty toe
Upon our cropped-lawned island home.
You've got some hope, don't make me laugh
Or I'll shove the junta up your ass!'
(Cheers.)
FEET: The Labour Party now demands
That we avenge this bloody deed
For bloody bloomin' bleeding war

Should we declare right now, no less
Foul and brutal aggression must not succeed,
Labour's not a pack of Tory weeds,
We'd be there, yes damn right we would.
What happened to 'Intelligence', they all dead?
Fingers up your assholes, blind dumb and deaf?
They've been telling us for years
They're going to give the mighty boot
What have you been doing love
Fiddling the books? Or plotting
With asslicker Nit, or Pimp the pontz, the crooks.
(Boos.)

SIR FISH FACE: I think we should ban Argentina
From entering the soccer World Cup
(Cheers, 'piss off', etc.)

NIT: I take great exception to Cheesy Feet
Accusing us of dragging our foot
When we were never even warned
Or if we were we didn't hear . . .
FO didn't tell us or the post went astray,
The lines were bad I believe that day,
Or else, oh yes we were away . . .
The file got buried or got mislaid
Oh, then we were on holiday . . .
Yes I remember that, the weather was fine . . .
You know how memos pile up high . . .
We did write a letter, I remember that . . .
But forgot to send it . . . The last chap was a prat.
But you know what we do with prats
Or silly buggers who make a balls,
We give the bastards the bloody sack
And they sleep it off in the House of Lords.
Anyway who are you to talk
In your worn-out elbows and smelly cords?!
You march against the nuclear bomb! ('Shame, shame.')
I've seen you stride with long-haired poofs
All the way to Aldermaston! ('Disgusting!')

MAGGOT: Can you imagine old Feet in the shop

24

When we'd come back to check the stock
He'd have the whole damn country in shock!
('Bravo!' Cheers!)
REASON: Surely, before we shed young blood
We must seek an ointment for the wound.
To heal must be then paramount
No more killing, not quite so soon
('Bollacks', 'appeaser', 'coward', etc.)
There must be time, no blood's been shed
Not one young English life's been lost
You seek a medicine for the sore
Not hack it with a bloody knife.
All human flesh belongs to God
You take one life, you take the world
Did Jesus say, 'Throw your stones first,
Those who are innocent of any sin.'
('Balls', 'Rubbish', 'Coward', 'Appeaser'.)
The world's become a tinder-box
You set a match and watch it flare
Death has become a TV screen
That we watch from our soft armchairs
('Sit down', 'Piss off', 'Left-wing pontz'.)
If you can call yourself Christians
If you believe in Christ our Lord
Then you will seek the bloodless way
Not solve it with a flaming sword.
('Commie', 'Bollacks,' etc.)

The Conqueror

SAILOR 1: Dear Janet, love, we're there, it's cold
We do six-hour shifts, I'm bored
Scotland lost the match we hear
There's not much else I can report.
SAILOR 2: Dear Sheila, still cleaning my gun
I'd love a decent cup of tea
Or even read the daily *Sun*,
You know, we still ain't killed anyone.

25

SAILOR 3: Dear Rita, there's not much about
        We saw a couple of old freights
        A sitting duck . . . but couldn't shoot
        The sods were outside the TEZ.
SAILOR 4: Dear Doreen, still feeling so proud
        But I can't wait to see their ships
        It's dark and silent as the grave
        I'm dying for us to make a hit.
SAILOR 5: Dear Mum, we don't know what's going on
        We hear no news except the crap
        They send us from HQ at home
        And politicians' daily chat.
SAILOR 6: Dear Judy, I don't want to kill
        I can't imagine what it's like
        The waves are like giant hills
        The sub feels like a block of ice.
COMMAND: Two-hundred-mile Exclusion Zone
        A lot of bloody bollacks that
        To steam around and watch the buggers
        Stick their tongues out, safe and fat,
        Hold on, we've had a signal here
        'Go out and sink a bloody ship'
        'Which one?' 'Who cares, just something near
        You've got to make a bloody hit'
        There's nothing in our target now!
        'The other sub will make the kill'?
        Give us a chance, we'll look around
        We'll get some juicy Argy ship
        Chock full of arms and fighting men.
        'Westminster wants some action' . . . Shit
        We've got our hands tied by the law.
        Can we attack them from the rear
        When they're outside the lines *you* draw?
        That just ain't cricket, is it dear?
        Or they may say, and it will be true,
        Britain does not rule the waves
        She simply waives the bloody rules!

Wait, hold on . . . just hang about
I'm picking up a distant tune
Let's go to periscope depth and peek . . .
A silhouette against the moon . . .

PIMP: (On phone) Hello, hello, Maggot, that you?
And how are things at home, my dear?
I'm chatting up old Cowboy Joe
And it could be that peace is very near.
MAGGOT: Hello, Pimp, speak up you drip
And don't believe all that you hear
Those greasy wogs are cunning sods
With all their talk of peace plans now
That our Task Force is bloody there.
PIMP: Well, to spell it out, the sods agreed,
Immediate cease fire, number one . . .
And then withdraw all Argy troops . . .
That's what we want to flaming hear
A third party to govern it,
While we thrash out conflicting views
And then the Islanders to have a say
Before the final solution day . . .
Well, it's not bad, is it, what d'ya think?
MAGGOT: What do I think . . .? It bloody stinks
Who cares about the rotten Islanders!
It's not what this is all about,
You stupid simpering silly pontz.
You think the wishes of those few
Will dictate how and what we do
We're not negotiating with them
It's us, Great bloody Britain mate
It's our corn that they stepped upon
You think we're going to war for them?
Spending four million quid a day
For eighteen hundred Bills and Ben!
PIMP: I know, I know, but still they say
Their wishes will be . . . etc. . . . .
And they can make peace this very day

27

It's up to us, they've cleared the decks
What shall I say ma'am . . .
Can I say . . . yes?

MAGGOT: No, no, no, no, no and no!
And that does not quite spell out yes.

PIMP: But ma'am, they have agreed our points . . .
Old Cowboy's flogged himself to death
We've been up all night . . .
For nearly a week . . .
A hot line between Joe and them . . .
We've squeezed the best possible deal . . .
Squeeze any more the marrow is next . . .
Give them a morsel . . .
Don't put it to the test . . .
They'll withdraw . . . we've won
Talk terms . . . no blood behind a desk . . .

MAGGOT: Tell Cowboy Joe, I need a fight
He needs it too, expose the sore
That may spread inside the flanks
Of England if we have no war
There's twenty-eight thousand Brits
On whom the world's eyes hold in awe
Are we going now to turn around,
Say, 'Sorry, lads, false alarm'?
Tell Cowboy, if we do then, farewell,
England falls to Socialist claws
Who will tear our land apart
Then who will support his Cruise missiles
Planted like teeth in our fair land
To scare off the Russian Bear
Or bite any invading hand?

PIMP: But then we're nearly almost there . . . !
What can I say then when they ask
What did your old Iron Lady think
Of our strong plan we made for peace?

MAGGOT: Stop whining, you sickening spineless wimp,
Oh God if only I had men around
And not this pair of leaking drips

That dribble daily in my mind.
Tell Cowboy I support *his* wars
Prop up *his* Nicaragua
Ignore his murder squads he sends
To clean up vile El Salvador
So screw this pissy peace plan, Pimp!

PIMP: OK ... I see the danger, ma'am ...
The troops return ... the drooping flags
No 'knees up, Mother Brown' in pubs
or clinking glasses in Buck House
No medals, no heroes lined up ...
Before the Nation's TV screens
No celebration of the deed
That spells out British victory
No revenge for the filthy slur
No hands in mouths waiting for news
No photos in the *Daily Muck*
Of Tommies clambering up hills
With smiling faces, British flags
Atop a craggy mount ...
No Islanders with whoops and cries
And cream teas for the hungry lads
Wide-angle lens of history
Being made by Fleet Street hacks
Who follow us with hungry lens
Ready to frame for all the world
The conquered lying in the dust
And Maggot Scratcher raised up high
And then, vote Tory ... written in the sky.

MAGGOT: A teardrop now steals from my eye
Oh, Pimp, for once you now speak true
At last, you see the truth at last
At long last you must see our cause
Thank God, the scales fell from your eye
You see, we must defend the state,
Not just some piece of rock with sheep
Dropping their rotund turds so thick
Or gentle Islanders shedding wool

29

Or rocking chairs for weary feet.
It's England, now at last you scan
The breadth of history ... The pulse
Of England must be strong, we *must*
Punish those who commit wrong ...
You know we've got them beat,
We paid the deposit ... Let's just complete.

PIMP: So what shall I tell Cowboy Joe?
They're sewing up the peace plan now.

MAGGOT: Say you couldn't get through,
You know the phones are always bad
By then we'll scuttle their little 'plan'
But make up a tale for the man.
(She hangs up.)

PIMP: Now I shall have to lie *again*
She always leaves me in the shit!
Oh well, it's nothing really new
Not when you're taught by the master bitch.
(Into phone) Hello Joe, how are you and how's the wife?
Listen, I can't get through right now ...
Nobody home, and embassies are closed ...
Weekends, you know, nobody works ...
Yes, the plan seemed fine to me
A hiccup perhaps just on one word?
What word is that they want to change ...?
'Wishes' ... to 'Aspirations' on the clause ...
Oh well, I'll have to call HQ
To see if 'aspirations' now will do
I know it's only just one word,
I know that time is running out
But we must analyse the sound ...
Weigh it carefully on the scales
Make sure we have value for a pound
I'll call you back without delay
OK? ... and, er ... have a nice day.

CHORUS: Now you see and now you don't
Imagine pounding on the rocks

A score of Harriers now unleashed
Shredding their targets like angry hawks
Then sweeping into the sky
Dissolving in a womb of cloud
Only the deep and throaty sound
Is heard as it again prepares
And down down it dives
Ploughing up earth rocks and trees
And sending fear into our enemy
Who cower, trembling hair on end
Affrighted by this show of strength
Watch them as their spines will bend
Beneath the blast of British breath
Hot, fierce as raging angry lion
Protecting her young cubs from death.

Lunch at Chequers

MAGGOT: We've not much time, the sands are running out
And at the end we'll be checkmate
By compromise and deals, my friends,
Unless we give the most almighty clout.

TELL: (Off, the war) Damn it all, we're hitting the buggers
hard
All day we rained down great dollops of pain
We attacked again and yet again
Port Stanley never will look quite the same
Our chaps are doing all they can but
If the buggers stay outside the line
The boxing match is fought with gloves,
Let's get them off and get some knuckles
Cracking on the swine . . .
WOODY: Hear bloody hear . . . What! Bloody shame
I call it . . . sod it, let's clout the buggers
As you say, knock one off and they'll not
Come out to play another day . . .

MAGGOT: Trouble is they have accepted all our terms

The very minimum we would accept,
They have by now accepted, bar one word
One bloody word will be the straw
To break the camel's back. That word
Will not go down, not if we choose
Not to accept their peace-meal stew.
But once they inform Joe that it's on
We can't then change our minds and say
It's off . . . Can we . . . How say you, Tell?

TELL: Bloody hell, that's what I bloody say
Damned good lamb New Zealand eh!
That's it . . . buy British or nearly . . . tasty . . . what!

MAGGOT: Have some mint sauce, Tell . . . Yes can we
Say it's off? I mean, can we say, sod off!
Too late, the balloon's gone up?

WOODY: Smash the buggers, in or out the bloody Zone
Reclaim what's ours, if we don't we'll be
A right example to the rest, besides
We could then test our toys, warn Russia too,
We'll make an example of all those that
Think the Lion is just a sleeping cat
I'm dying to see how Sea-cat missiles
Fare and Tiger-fish torpedoes blasting
Holes, at half-a-million quid a time,
Bit costly that, but think of all the orders
We will get once they see them in the act
Tests and war games aren't the same
As seeing them work on living game.

TELL: Right, let's get to work, let's heat it up.

MAGGOT: Oh Tell, you speak the words I want to hear
Where can we clout the sods before they
Crawl behind the UN skirts in fear?

TELL: Sink a bloody Argy ship!
Hit them where it hurts the most
A packed full, well armed with young men,
A thousand maybe more, hit in one below
Condemn to darkness their young pride
Then watch them cave in when they feel our punch

You take one out, you take them all
They'll be on their knees, you'll see.
MAGGOT: Oh Tell, I'm thrilled with ecstasy
More lamb? Go on, it's piping hot
Some roast, 'fraid they're just overdone,
Now go on. . . . sink one!? Bloody hell.
Then it's all over really? You think so, Tell?
TELL: Could be very well . . . They'll see
That we mean business . . . won't risk
Coming out and lose an arm, mabe a leg
We've got them well and truly pegged.
MAGGOT: They wouldn't attack *our* ships, would they, Tell?
TELL: Can't see how, we know their strength
Got all the facts, thanks to old Joe
Who fed us all the info that we need
To know, give us the word, let's go.
MAGGOT: You don't need me, just do your work
I'm right behind you lads you know.
WOODY: We've trailed a lovely Argy ship
Stacked full as Tell has just described
We've got them in our sights . . . could
Blast them now to kingdom come.
One battleship just steaming on
With two destroyers by her side
Like taking two alsatians for a walk,
They'll bark a bit maybe
But won't do much when they will see
Their master's bleeding guts,
But then they're just outside the TEZ.
Please change the rules and then you'll see,
Madam, a swift sharp British victory.
MAGGOT: Can we do that? So easily.
Or won't it seem in the world's eyes
That we have been a mite extreme?
WOODY: No, bloody hell, let's say we saw them
Start to stray across the line . . .
TELL: They posed a threat to us, our boys,
Were steaming straight just hours away

33

We had to sink the bugger without delay!

WOODY: They're bristling with fire power ma'am,
With two missile-packed escort destroyers
Like armed guards ready to defend the boss
Who himself carries fifteen six-inch guns.
We had to sink it or face our loss
God knows how many lives we'll save.

MAGGOT: You think we'll save lives?

WOODY: Of course, we'll stop the war
They'll have no bottle left to fight!

TELL: Attack them now, before they go,
There may not be a chance again
And then we'll bite our nails and sigh
Oh why didn't we do it then, you'll moan.

MAGGOT: What do you mean, 'before they go'?

TELL: Well . . . info is, that they're heading back home
They're on a track you see, two-ninety degrees,
Between ten and eleven knots, we'll lose them
Though we've had them in our sights
A day or more, we're waiting for the light.

MAGGOT: Sunlight?

TELL: No green, give us the green one, madam!

MAGGOT: I may say, now forgive me if I winge
That to sink a bloody ship (sailing away
You say) in cold blood gives me just a twinge
I know it's right, I know . . . but when I think
Of hundreds of young boys, they could be ours,
Stopped dead and floating in the drink
It does . . . just for a second . . . make me think . . .

TELL: Don't! . . . ma'am don't, be hard as steel
The Iron Lady, come, not brass not tin
Like leaking oil can in *Wizard of Oz*,
But iron! Rigid, hard, inflexible . . .
Your reputation earned the whole world wide
The Iron Lady with a velvet glove??
No! Iron fist to match a steely heart.

MAGGOT: (Inspired) Then sink the bloody sod, that's what I
say

We'll change the engagement rules . . . OK.

TELL: We'll drink to that.

WOODY: Can't wait to give the bloody orders
They will be pleased, they're getting
Bored sailing around the endless seas.

MAGGOT: What shall we say? Let's all decide
To tell the same story, on the day.

TELL: Get Nit . . . to extricate his tongue
With due respect from out your ass,
And tell the press and parliament . . .
'A heavily armed surface attack group
Close to the Exclusion Zone, was closing
In on our Task Force . . . only hours away . . .
Ignore them at our peril, that's what he'll say.

MAGGOT: But that's not strictly true, they're sailing away
You say, some forty miles south-west of the Zone
Can't we sink something deep inside . . .
That we can certainly justify . . .

TELL: There's bugger all . . . They've kept outside
And this one's closest, ma'am, and soon
That won't be there much longer . . .
Look, if we don't hit it now
We'll have to sink them in their ports
And claim we heard them start their engines
And posed a threat to our Task Force!
And how do you know that they
Won't turn . . . How do you know it ain't
One big bluff . . . They calm us down
And then one night ka-blam and blast
And British lads are feeding sharks.

MAGGOT: Those last words indeed touched my heart
Of course my woman's soul trembled a jot
At thoughts of bloody bodies
All unseamed and torn apart
And widowed mothers clutching their
Now fatherless sons and daughters
Must admit since our wombs carry flesh
And blood and watch the shoot become a plant

35

Must admit that for a moment I did hesitate
Forgot that I was iron, instead a mum
Worried when child is late . . .
What's the time?

WOODY: It's one o'clock

MAGGOT: (Recovering) Then give the order . . . Let it be
swift.
Anyway those bastards started it
Let them now take the consequence . . .

CHORUS: Now cast your mind o'er wind-swept choppy seas
Where ships lay waiting rocking to and fro
A great armada, armed with might and men
Who wait, alert, primed ready to unleash
The power that is awesome coiled within
Imagine now the crew. Some sleeping, some awake
Their radar scanning thunderous clouds,
Some writing letters home to their sweethearts
And others still deciphering strange codes
Which spell the fate of those who live or die,
Some playing cards, some singing old pop songs
While others dream of clutching their warm wives
And in those cloudy seconds before sleep and wake
Imagine they will turn around and hold their mate.
For some, alas, this night will be their last
Their young unfinished lives will be reclaimed
Within the freezing sea, their unknown graves.

The Conqueror

COMMAND: Up periscope . . . OK, we see them clear
Action station . . . all at high alert
It's nearly fifteen hundred hours, Sunday May the Second.
That's nearly seven o'clock back home
Opening time in all the pubs
We'd wander down and have a pint
Maybe play a game of darts or two
I've got her in my sights, ten thousand tons

Of steel, at least one thousand Argy men
Just slowly ploughing up the sea
A steady speed of ten to thirteen knots,
Like some old carthorse pulling reins of foam
But at her side two dangerous chaperons
Ready to destroy with claws
That reach into the sky some twenty miles
Seek out your heat and then like bloodhounds
Hold your course until they taste your meat.

SAILOR: They're only blokes like us ... don't fire ...
Not fire one off ... like in cold blood ...
Not warn 'em first and fire a warning shot?
Like shift over boys, you're getting close
It's not the Second World War ... is it?

COMMAND: We're now four thousand yards away from her
Portside and steering the same course
A wicked sea and choppy waves
Some four or five metres high and fog,
Standby and fire one off ... OK ...
We'll use Mark-8 torpedoes, they're safe
Dependable, and should get there on the day.

SAILOR: The wind's now blowing fifty knots
Across the raging, icy sea ...
To put a man alive in that
Would quietly send him first to sleep
A few more minutes he might live
Dreaming in his icy bed
Until the cold has drained his heart
And death sucks out his last breath.

COMMAND: Fire one. Forty-three seconds it should take.

SAILOR: God ... Let them not feel any pain ...!
Oh Jesus Christ ...

(Silence of forty seconds. A sea of anxious faces.
One face in pain. Will it hit?)

COMMAND: ... A hit! ...

(Total cheering ... back slapping ... One man still
frozen in his agony ... Sounds die out, just the faces
moving in celebration. Slow fade.)

CHORUS: The first torpedo pierced the ship like
It was made of butter – sunk right through
Then tore inward and upward through
Four steel thick decks ... It spun its deadly
Groove ... It sunk itself into its guts
And ripped its soul apart ... The old ship
Then simply turned around and died ...
The lights went out ... just silence ...

(Darkness ...)

Dead men were everywhere, in bits.
A piece of arm and here a leg ...
Upon the deck a figure covered in burning oil
All black and running as the heat roasted
His flesh. Three hundred and thirty sailors died at once ...
The others dragged their shredded flesh
To rafts to face the icy sea, thirty-six hours more
Or less ... The conscripts, boys of eighteen years
Stayed disciplined and kept their nerve
Each one ready to sacrifice himself to
Help an ally or a wounded friend. At
Seventeen O one just one hour more. The *Belgrano*
Sank stern first beneath the waves.

SAILOR: The dead men did not pay the price
Of peace, for others died the selfsame
Way, when two days later in revenge
Our ships were sunk, and many died
Or were simply burned alive ...

SAILOR: Somebody threw the first stone
When the *Belgrano* was going home.

(On screen the following image: 'I would do it again'
... Margaret Thatcher. Blackout.)

MASSAGE

CHARACTERS

DAD
MUM
MAN

DAD: Simple-minded jerks and fuckwits/mouths agape and crutch on fire/wiggle ass and 'love you's dripping out their stupid lips/while rock and rolling down the grotty disco/dressed like freaks that from your worst of nightmares grew living flesh and blood/but there the semblance ends/for they to us are like to chalk and cheese/to life and death/from wholesome *homo sapiens* to thing that from a womb wast nuked and came out like the devil had distributed his evil seed within/I saw one strolling down our natural homely street/our strip of sanctuary lined with trees and turds of dogs so neatly dropped/with wholesome pub on corner/saw this thing as if from outer space/hair spiked like porcupines/and he thick wedged in shoes totters his hair pinned nose into our suburb haven/brains of ants/they follow the dull parade of clones/the dyed and painted saboteurs of all that's holy/the wreck of our permissive state zipped out on grass and smack/and I don't mean a romp in epping forest with your favourite tart for a taste of slap and tickle but the shit they shove into their empty skulls/so roomy that it needs the constant kick of noxious dope to prove that to itself it's still alive.

MUM: More tea, Frank?

DAD: Yeah, pour out the nectar sweet balm and elixir/the tonic for our dried-up british throats/the balm that greets our tired morning eyes/when rising from our stinking pits in balham, kent or palmers green/prepare ourselves for one more day of shirk and strike/the brown and steaming stew doth re-invigorate our will/stiffen our pride and puts the sparkle back in our jaundiced eyes/that magic brew/that simple british leaf/that greets us late at night before thick slumber wraps us up/a fag just puffed before/put out the light and then put out your light/oh! the bubble gurgles and it glob glob globules out the old brown pot/that heart-rending and happy sight/old browny on the table top/the pride of england/ne'er feel the stroke of bitter loss or strife whiles cuppas will be there to

41

dull the razor's edge/and as I say farewell to this fair state/let
my last taste of england be/a nice old brown and sweetened
cup a tea/(drinks).
Bleedin' hell . . . it's bloody cold, mate!

In massage parlour

MUM: So many years have passed since first I found a way to
honest toil by doing what I like, that is to squeeze the miles of
cock that sausage-like have passed between these walls/so
many cocks so many shapes/some large/some small/some
tall and thin have strutted and have heaved their silver pearls
upon this well-worn slab/they stand up to attention, ready
and alert and pass themselves to me, in trust that I will shed
their load and send them out into the world all light and fresh/
and ready now to face the thing in semi-detached bliss/with
me their fantasies are now fulfilled/I am the shepherdess that
tends the sheep/and milks the cows, for that is how it seems/
pour out and squeeze the nectar and the pain/I'll rent my
hand and voice/my subtle touch to their world-weary aching
ends of flesh/just aided by the finest oil/I baste their swollen
joints, caress and soothe, tickle and pinch and faster now and
faster doth my hand like a pneumatic pump explore the riches
down and bore and drill until the hit. The target, solid gold/
bull's eye, then whoosh/the spray ascends as showers on an
april morn/some kleenex doth remove the clues then off they
go these valiant and most noble men of england/to return to
their dull wives with sour miens/their nagging and unwholesome shrill/who frame their dried-up lips into a ring of woe
and pour the doldrum, poison and demands of married life/
that rings and contracts they believe have given them/

MAN: (Stripping) Oh woe is me let me escape and be soft putty in
your hands/I cast myself like ulysses when he, the sirens'
filthy sound did drive him total mad/give me a massage,
sherry, if that's your name and make it topless now as well.

MUM: For topless as you know another fiver must be paid/plus
fiver for relief/the oil or powder/choice is yours/or take the
total lot/be bold the day is yours/invest another ten and I will

42

shed my briefs/those gossamer sweet drawers and shall arise like venus striding forth/naked as the day/you'll have me quivering there as succulent as aphrodite and guileful as the sphinx/my hands will touch you like you never knew/you'll writhe like quicksilver between my flesh/I am the virtuoso of the wank but lest you should be tempted and ten pounds more at that/there is a treat in store which I reserve for only those I like/the special crest of all the rest/the summit and the peak to make your very bones cry out and shriek/

MAN: Pray gentle nymph/thou sweet and foul/thou noxious temptress in these cells of red/tell me thou devil what treasure might I avail myself without being cleaned of all my pence and save a buck or two/so that my kids at school might feed and not face hunger by my lustful greed/

MUM: Fear not my gentleman nor seek high favours at low cost by sentimental guile/with chatter of the hardship and the face of little kids to float with pinched and hungry face before my woman's eyes/I know these cool male tricks to make a score with chicks with cheap words forged in heat and lust, and not be paid the price for my soft woman's paradise/the cost is high/if you cannot afford then stay at home with tv on and pine/watch your old mate undress to bed/and as your eyes do scan that worn-out wreck/those gnarled legs and ass spread out to bust and think yuk no sweet thrill but only wasted life ahead/

MAN: O honest whore/those words that trickle from your oral, smart and lash me with the stings of truth/I pay much more to keep the shriek at home whose constant open mouth *keeps* wolf at door/plus two fat bonny brats which tho' I love, between the three of them, they suck the life from out my craw.

MUM: What does she do for you? Does she caress you like I do? Does she anoint your prick with oil that's precious and perfumed in shades of musk to make it glisten like a rain-lashed oak or carved by michelangelo all knarked and swollen/knotted and thick proud with mushroom head glutted in blood the rich red ruby racing rampant to the crest/transporting lust to the nerve centre of it all/the emperor of the body/the stalwart rising beast/the hungry eyeless mouth/

the snake about to spit/straining at the leash above two
mighty balls rich and filled up/those oysters primed and
ready to give up their dewy pearls/I, me my woman's sting/
my soft electric thing I fantasize in you to make such hard-ons
as you never knew you had/I live to make you glad/that god
shoved on your end this whisper shred of flesh/this toy/this
morsel that the more you eat/the more it grows in solid hunky
meat/

MAN: (Dawning) Aah! So there's the treat!

MUM: A mouthful of deep throat
      You'll be a dog in heat
      (She takes it out and performs it.)

Home

DAD: What can I say as I return to this soft womb/the triumph of
     my years of slog/and view upon the coloured screen the won-
     ders of the human race/and as the old bird dishes up the magic
     of her *cordon bleu* I slosh it down with half a pint to take away
     the taste of mush/my cock sits all quite comfortable and small
     at peace and smiling in his sable sack/digesting pleasure from
     the afternoon when like a tiger sprung he from his slack and
     concertinahed shell to march forth into action ... all pell-mell/
     she sucked me like a good'un just to tell you straight/my life
     felt like the source of it was drawn and slid along the tunnel of
     love, my prick/it was the rocket ship that made its vertical
     ascent and soared upwards to heaven/my piece of red-hot
     rocket stood alert on pad/fuelled up for scorching take off/
     octane blast/all tight and proud/come on and press that
     magic switch/the button that would send us spitting into
     space/would send the plume all white and shining into orbit/
     at last as if my flesh was inside out and raw/as if some fruit was
     peeled exposing succulently its juicy meat/I felt the tremor
     start like acres down and deep/in the inferno where the ache is
     dim, deep down in the abyss where chasms stretch and moun-
     tains crack/where rocks begin to seethe and boil/
     and lava bakes just aching to escape and pour into the air its
     bottled boiling snakes of white-hot lust/so there I was/it cost
     a bundle/topless, bottomless too/I had the lot/the works/the

oil and french or gobble at the end/straining at the leash/
buttocks compressed almost to billiard balls/I turned myself
like inside out/and then like mount vesuvius started to spout/
MUM: More tea, love . . .?
DAD: But hush, here is the thing from whom I hide the best part of
my sting . . .

Yeah, throw some in and bung us too some holy ghost that I
might then anoint with perfumed marmalade the crusty bread
and wash it down with magic rosy lee . . . nice tea . . .
(Praise.)

Job Satisfaction

MUM: Last night I had a busy time I tossed off seven was fucked
by three/and gave head to two more/so tired but satisfied
with work/my old man in armchair all well and truly smug at
home, in bliss with kids the shiny offspring of our connubial
lust, tho' lately his once almighty hard-on has hit the dust/
which to tell true has been some small relief to a girl who is all
day engaged in giving same at work called 'on the game'/tho'
game it hardly is/more like a slog to get through the assembly
line of dirty dogs.

Legal Whoring

MUM: So you who scorn and look askance/you opened up your
legs when first you saw your mystery as capital/and made
yourself into a painted bait to catch the slippery eel/my cunt
and woman's touch it's true I sell but you would not give all
until you were provided with the means of living well! You
ensnared your men and threw your golden lassoo in the air/
but first you saw the lucre in the bank/the sexual capitalist
would tease and goad/say not now darling, later on/would
pout and be all coy in lacy frills/glossy lips and soft perfume in
rolling hills/would lie in wait tarantula to catch her prey and
milk him slowly/that's your way.

You lived in quilted eiderdowns and china sets/a bedroom
spare for passing friends/a dog called captain runs amok
among the old man's shirts and sox/you so faithfully daily
wash/you lucky bitch/for treasure lines your flock-lined

walls/your tasteful three-piece suite in lounge and rocking
chair for the old man/a ton of babies' things to wash which
stink/au pair bungs it in wash machine/the dryer too/oh
super darling . . . ain't she cute/your baby's sweet/she's only
two/samantha . . . oh that's lovely/shit! she pissed all over
my best suit/the garden's coming on this year/we're grow-
ing pansies and freesias dear/you playing bridge this
afternoon/oh no, today the kids come home from school/I
love the white brocade/the lacy curtains look so fresh and
frothy/don't, captain! Get out in the garden/samantha! don't
you give the dog a hard-on/leave him dear/I know its pink/oh
shit, the cat's shit in the sink/brr! brr! It's mum, yes I'm ok I
just don't know what to cook today/he's getting bored/what
shall I make/I know he works hard . . . 'Evening dear' . . . a
peck and then the gin appears/nice day darling . . . 'not too
bad' I'm bored to death/it's just like dad and mum when I was
young/the same desireless dreary death and boredom dan-
druff and bad breath/is this the life/is this for me/you chose it
dear/you held the key/to puss in bank and made him pay if he
was to unlock your safe/you wannit then you work and say/
my pussy's sold not given away a ring a house a signed
contract/he sweats and every day he will regret/he's bored/
tough tits mister/pay you wretch/she's whored her arse to
you you git/you loved it once/you're bored right now/too bad
pal/you're stuck to the cow you wanna scram? It'll cost you
dear/she'll suck your money better than she ever ate the thing
that got you into trouble mate! She'll drain you/look she's
good at it/she's just a high-class whore you git/she steals from
men and makes them pay whenever she gives puss away/she
does it legal like and smiles in church while ma and pa cry like
two jerks.

The British Way of Life

DAD: I'm up/I am the british worker bred from the holy lineal
strain/the viking and the dane have put the good old british
rich blood in our veins/we fought and smashed the filthy hun/
painted the world red coast to coast/from zanzibar to taj
mahal/the pucker sahib was master there/we taught the

46

darkies who's the boss/erased the aboriginal and tossed the black man back into his shanty town to make south africa a jewelled crown/we showed the pakkies how to play a game of cricket the english way the world we made a safer place for christians and our wives to saunter in/and showed them jesus, taught them sin/and watched the millions come pouring in/ and I mean pounds not bleeding wogs/not stinking krauts or dirty frogs/but good hard british notes/a pound was worth a pound in them good days/nowadays inflation runs so fast/ you're running like diarrhoea flows out your arse/in case you shit your wages out before you've time to buy a snout/before you said hey! twenty smokes it's up again/before you've time to nosh your grub, so mum and I we wolf it down whenever we go into town/in case the waiter comes on strong and says hey mate your steak's gone up/it's one quid more than when you stepped inside the door/in olden days an indian was just a darkie in a big wigwam/but now the high street chimes with names like taj mahal and tandoori/with eastern star and bengali/the mob have come across to sink the nation in a stink of pancake rolls and popadoms/hot curries that can make you shit from islington to oxford street/the mob have come to take revenge and take this island back with them/they'll stuff us full of curry that one day just one almighty fart will blow away this septic isle/we'll float in seas like some almighty turd you sometimes see bobbing its little head in the wine-dark sea/ whole streets and boroughs pound with drums and cassette decks the size of tanks they'd carry on their shoulders like a little kid you'd give a ride/they look like blackened martians skating down with earphone stuck around their frizzy crown/ it's dangerous now to step outside/in your own manor lest you collide with king kong doing fifty miles an hour. Put the telly on, love/I'd love to see old farty licking arses clean of some old has-been celebrity.

The Whore's Story or One's Story

MUM: I scanned the western world for cock that gallops at a lifted frock/we know it fades/'tis temporary/that's why we add the touch of lie/with cream and powder/pout in pink/coyly resist

47

in satin and stink of musk behind the ears/and make them think we're little dears/small pussies cradled in white pants as soft as marshmallows and tame those hot red monsters out for game/but cock must be attached to rocks that sparkle/rock-hard stocks and shares in bank/securities and no small wanker out to use us for his selfish gain/our box is assets/truly stored we are the sexual overlords/the sexual capitalists of the world/so whore and housewife are the same/they both go out to work for gain/the one in hard cash for quick time/the other will wait until what's yours is mine.

Come to me, come to *me*, you men of rock whose thighs are weighted down with balls so heavy under-used and bored/come to me at massage house/and let my hand play out a tune/that on your flute will make you swoon/and if you want the topless too/and special bottomless as well, a tenner more will see the sight that men would die for/rot in hell even to glimpse/the shining tips and ornaments/the swelling vales and creamy sponge of silky breasts and as I plunge your cock into my mouth, my tongue will round your head enfurl and part my standing legs for you to dip your hungry hands into/I'll squirm and wiggle, pulse and twist/I'll bite your steaming bulging prick/I'll take it deep down far inside my throat/I'll chew it softly tender, stroke with oil the smouldering shaft and lick the veins in the underhalf, running my tongue along its ridge/dip the tip into the cyclops eye/while far below you crush and scoop my creamy cerements/my holy fruit my pomegranates/ripe raw figs, your fingers squeeze my slit and dig/dig down, dig deep dig far as if to rip the fruit from off its branch/and then I squeeze your thickened shaft caress your swollen balls and sense the pulse begin to start/the heavy blood-swelled prick grows to its final ramrod juicy stick/the spunk begins to rise/my mouth goes faster faster now/the knob inflates its crest like some huge flower opened up/your fingers still like snakes dart in and out and crawl inside my silky satin mouse/oh yes the flood hot thick and white burst through the tunnel in fiery wet hot sticky spouts/in gooey creamy bursts/the gates break/the flood aches through/in spurts of warm soft silvery glue/oh comey gurgle gulp and

48

slurp/hmmm! hmmm! ... swallow hot vats of semen down and lick it clean/while up above your face, serene like now the moon was free from clouds/and smiled with silly cheesy grin/meanwhile I felt it shrink again and small like going back to its cocoon/he gets up, smiles and y-fronts he puts on/he reckons he's had a tasty one/I send him out into the world all nice for wifey/stroked and spoiled/was that all right ducky ... 'yeah great' his old lady at home would hate to do the things I do/would say I'm just a filthy whore/but her old man comes back for more/

Transactions

MAN enters massage parlour.

MUM: Hello, ducky/seen the menu?
      Hand relief ... ten quid.

MAN: Oh yeah.

MUM: Topless relief. Fifteen quid.

MAN: Oh yeah.

MUM: Top- and bottomless, twenty quid.

MAN: Oh yeah.

MUM: French twenty-five and full french thirty.

MAN: Oh yeah.

MUM: Spanish thirty and greek forty.

MAN: Oh yeah.

MUM: Greek and french forty-five.

MAN: Oh yeah.

MUM: All-in fifty.

MAN: Oh yeah.

MUM: Reverse, greek and french fifty-five.

MAN: Mmm.

MUM: Reverse, greek, french and spanish, plus bondage seventy.

MAN: Mmm ... what's spanish?

MUM: Between the boobs, dear.

MAN: And excuse me, but greek?

MUM: Anal love, love.

MAN: What's french then?

MUM: Oral.

MAN: And full french?

MUM: Oral and cum in the mouth, dear.

MAN: I see.

MUM: All right, dear ... what would you like?

MAN: Tell you what ... I'd like a touch of spanish and a slice of greek and then spring into a double reverse with a piece of french easin' off into a whisper of bondage/a grab of relief and relax into bottomless sex whip out into greek and ending in a full french at the end.

MUM: I can't do that, can't go from greek to french/I can go from french to greek or you could have a two-girl bottomless-topless hand relief into bondage. A bit of tv french and whip down into greek finishing up at athens.

MAN: Ok. I'll have that. How much?

MUM: A hundred pounds all-in but I'll do it for fifty.

MAN: Ok. I paid my gelt and went into a dark red room/my flies were bursting in anticipation and I sunk into my reveries as I undid my pants/I stood in my knickers with my great sausage squashed tight and making it stiffer, I looked in the mirror and thought it quite nice as I heard muzak trickling through the flock-lined walls/there was kleenex in the wastebin, I unpeeled my pants and out it sprang like a hoop or like a grey-hound sniffing around for meat and wondering what to do ...

Whore's Life

MUM: Do you think I like my cunt used like a sink/a vile cesspit/a bin of stink/a crock of rotting sperm-choked drain/repository for all the pain of man who comes so stupid in with breath of rot and yellow grin/who stumbles over in the dark, his alcoholic brain in nerve-torn shreds/the last bits in the lower self/the basement of his mind/let's have a fuck/he sees a picture in the shit-heap room he occupies of tits and panties black/stockings held up by straps and open thighs and arse to clutch/he sees the morbid tattered pictures in his head when boredom, drunken conscious stunned only a walking thing that lives to eat and fuck and sometimes shit/a thing that staggers out at night with mates dead equal in thick leer and hate of women, soft things animals and tears/and hate of love, people, earth and fears only that his cock/his filthy smegma tip won't stand up when his money's out/his heaving bloated corpse/his rotten evil smell/this junk of man/this piece of evil hell/still tries to get it up/still farts and burps 'oh fuck it, love, I can't get stiff . . . I think I boozed too much, oh shit . . . it's gone again, just hang about tell me some filthy stories to make it stiff and sprout'/ok. I tell him about whips and frightened teenagers well bound with leather straps/legs spread with downy dewy thatch/whose tears flood down and beg and cry/yet burn between their virgin mounds/for fingers, tongues and hard thick pricks to pound/she moans oh no! soft rosebud tits/small even slits he pulls apart/opens up the rose petals and peers inside the flower's heart/its stamens and its pollen exposed to the lurid eye/so whip the soft pink creature make her squeal/her soft pink arsehole makes you thrill and bend her over like an animal/examine all her sacred bits/ explore each part that once forbid and secret in the sanctuary of the shy/your cock grows fat by weaker creature's pain/the more it hurts the greater is your gain/you are now hero/ conqueror and proud/your prick runs rampant now and stiff the magic elixir for dick is kicking others/so hit and pinch/ slap hard and whip/her eyes they open wide and beg no more but this is sweet for you and then the thick hard shaft slides in the juicy glue and howl scream cry/oh god these sounds are paradise while down below the furnace is ablaze/your filthy dick's on fire now and shoots its steaming spunk along the trail/and shrivel slurp and slop/wipe off/'that's great, ta-da'/ you and your stink you gather up/open the door and into the night's old womb you're swallowed up and join the stream of human filth that teems along the gutter swill/

MAN: (Still waiting in parlour) So there I was/all waiting in my rose-hued room and cock as white and hard as marble/when I thought of all the lips and eyes and tits and thighs and all the sighs when hands clenched in the back row of john garfield's body and soul and shy to touch the crushy blouse whose swollen promontory housed within the stiffened bra the marsh-

mallow and squeezy tits with orbs so pink and delicate that
sneaked out when your hand would clutch the melting snow
and nipples sweet would peep between your fingers/saw her
knickers when in armchair's squelchy throne her knees so
high and eyes would dive down to those svelte and mossy
thighs/the inside of those legs/whose stockings clasped like
lizards' skins and fire glowing in the grate/would wonder as I
glimpsed the ivory veil/that masked the heavy squelchy mass
of sticky schoolboy dream/the pouring lovesick ecstasy/the
juicy runny fruit/the cocky cunt/the figgy rasp of hissy snaky
pungent hole/I would so calmly lift the gentle dress and wait
for her to stop my filth caress/just wanted now so much my
hand to glide right up to where the heat and scent and fantasy
collide and knees and squeeze and higher yet and no, her hand
has censored nothing. Still I slide now each new inch my itch-
hard hungry fingers scale the slope, another pulse of blood
pours in my prick to service what it hopes will be a fast inser-
tion into ecstasy/above the tongue twists round and now one
sucks and now one rolls the pink wet carpet out/she nibbles
tip of tongue and close tight eyes whose lashes like thin spi-
ders' legs crawl out her sweet mince pies and still/yet still
within the thunderstroke of drum pound heart/my hand still
scales the warm silk soft and creamy leg until just at the end of
stocking felt the flesh the narrow channel separating leg and
crutch and was a pearly bridge I scanned/oh sweet the heavy
pound of blood/my heart withstands the heavy thump/the
furious flow/I kiss the harder, flooding mouth and lips with
all the flesh my face can separate from skull as if by some
osmosis we conjoined or rocks whose atoms smashed into
each other's grip and now for all time are fixed/and so her lips
and mine were tight entwined who knows where hers begun
or where did mine/and then yes then the arched embrace/her
head pulled back/the other hand/rings her cotton waist/the
other like a filthy snake/dress now gathered up in folds like
ripples from a stone-pierced lake/so my hand was there along
the slippery vale/towards the honey of her soul/her squeezy
triangle of joy/and soon so soon I'd feel my fingers sense the
pertinent and thin silk ridge/and yes I'm holding harder yes

I'm near/my heart is flood in blood so red hot current thick
and then yes then/her crutch seemed almost now to lose itself
to me and slide towards my hand/my hand becomes my soul/
my hunger, my antennae to my lusts and greedy musts/is like
a taste or tongue/my hand becomes a stomach/starved and
hunger struck, and then yes then/just then, just when I was so
near and felt the heat/and sensed the peaty rich and swollen
sack/my hand and fingers traced its path/inch by inch/until
my fingers were in touch with velvet ambrosia and prick-
hungry lust/my hand then knew the end and the beginning/
knew that gold was there and waiting to be mined/I felt my
hand open and close around the gift/a sparrow settled in my
hand/and then like dream and ecstasy was in my palm which
bore the sweet stigmata of her love/my fingers became snakes
burrowing beneath the gauze/did lift the veil so tight and yet
just room enough/I pulled it back as if peeling a skin and felt
my fingers like hot knives into butter sinks/and so my fingers
sunk deep down and drunk like sponges parched and gasping
for her touch of soft underbellies of squids or persimmons that
break and crush open when ripe and squirt the too sweet juice
into your bite/

MUM: (Enters.) Hallo, love ... day-dreaming?

I do not ask for guts hung down in tresses bobbing in the
bubbly waves/I like my pricks hung stiff like some upright
and young spring rose/not shrivelled in a heap/cut off at root
by missile bullet or knife/you who squeal at this and yet con-
done the rats that chew upon your babies' limbs/the rats that
carry plague of hate/the filthy death's head shrieking death to
all/so all may be as dead as they/hate walks in petticoats and
skirts just as easily as khaki blood-stained trews/hate stems
from thick black bile that's boiled in witches' stew/
round the cauldron we will go/pour in frustration/dried-up
cunt that for a score of years was parched/and withered prick
that died unused and crushed between pinstripe and office
seat/balls hung like prunes or mouldy figs/throw in that too/
and to repression's smelly breath to season it/and then mean
withered fingers that never knew the soft caress/no never felt
the ache of sex/no never sweetened soft and pulpy parts with

awesome gift of life that pours from out the stem of love's caress / throw in the pot small wizened eyes that have the hate of basilisks / that hates the naked sight of god's pure fruit / the living flesh / pop in those fishy eyes and stir until it's thick and rich / then add now the viper's tongue / the bitter lashing whip of scorn / prejudice and hate / intolerance and greed to make this rot concoction into a rancid paste / tongue that ne'er knew peaceful balm of love or sounds to pour oil on the troubled seas / tongue that drinks from casks of wrath and spews out drivel shit and waste / words so vile like sink and shoot to kill / attack revenge / how dare you / splatter / tongues that consign young and brilliant downy boys to be drowning in blood and burning oil / if everyman's your son and brother / father too / how could you make your heap of evil stew you crock of filth / if you knew how a soft caress could calm and make the temple that you occupy god-filled, how would you then give words / orders to kill except you never knew / numb withered eyeless / senses buried in hard crusts of scarry tissue / leathern worn out / living at the end of life / the barest light from deadened batteries / so pour in all to make this soup of death / a mass of tangled limbs tossed in the bloody foam-flecked sea / my child and yours sinking down deep in gore / were it yours / were it yours / you filthy evil coward rot-gutted insult to a whore /

The Nature of Dirt

DAD: Oh that made a change from all the filth outpouring from my filthy gob / let's rather read the sunday press / regale ourselves with the minds of yobs / who talk more shit than ever was / flushed down my loo in the name of wit / let's cast my mind to other realms / like strolling down a country lane and pick blue-bells in velvet woods and feel the wind caress my brain / see fairies dancing on a brook where sunlight hits the rippling waves / should like to hike down endless roads / where summer paints a golden haze / nor feel the end will ever come / like those hot youthful endless days / so strolling through the blackberries and scratch my knees on thorny pricks and clutching wordsworth tenderly I lay beside a tickling brook / I

felt the grass caress my neck/saw mighty branches float and
sway/as if by indian eunuchs they were fanned to brush the
blowflies from my face/I lay and thought tho' half asleep I
heard the wind whisper sweet things/saw dancing pair of but-
terflies dissolve like snowflakes in the sky/which poured beneath my lazy lids/all blue then purple as thick sleep
poured over me in summer's heat/an aching slumber fell and
gently folded me into its spell/I sank like stardust in the sea/
or like a pebble thrown so eagerly by some small urchin/hits
the wave so hard and shatters crystal spray and then slowly it
sinks away/so sank I 'neath the sound of bells from distant
steeple/odd squawks/the ripple of a brook would talk and
distantly in summer haze some thrilling laughter blazed a
pathway to my hideaway/yet through the deep veil of my doze
heard sweet young schoolgirls far away rejoice in school-
work's end of day/the bells I heard chimed four the magic
hour that all children score upon their hearts for years/the teatime, four when all of england stops/forgets their fears lays
their hammer and their chisel down/even the hangman stops/
and says not now my friend/the noose will wait/the surgeon
deep inside the brain to brilliantly remove the source of pain/
he too will nevertheless stop and pause as he sees the theatre
clock strike four/

Down tools, down instruments/the nation breaks as if to
say, this special time of day we pray together/gently sip the
golden brew and know from queen to pauper up and down the
state this hot leaf will remove constraints/dissolve the walls/
we'll drink together, rich and poor/a nice old english cup of
char/I lay there so contented on my green and silken bed and
realized o wretch that I alone in the vast tapestry of england's
patchwork quilt/a little emblem stitched within its hills/will
not be there in village teashop/sanctuary/or even greasy alf's
café/to celebrate with all mankind/to be the vital link that
binds the souls of england/hold the teacup trembling to my
lips/close my eyes and taste sweet bliss/but this was not to be/
so I lay back letting the slumber dull the ache of quenching
that old taste I had and soon forgot/the voices grew and then I
as I was midway through oneiric land and like endymion to

sleep forever on his little grassy bank/deep in my dreams or so it seemed to me/I saw a vision slowly walk in schoolgirl tilted hat and thick pigtails/all glowing nubile and so virile, strong and bursting out their bodies like a song to nature/their cotton blouses bulged apart and pearly buttons seemed to pop as if like young spring roses could not be restrained from opening their petals to nature's gaze/their brown and tawny thighs like some great scythe cut through late summer's grass, knee high/they slashed their way leaving a trace of giggles hung upon the day/just like the wake rude ships upon the emerald green do make/so deep down in my hypnos cave/my lids stitched down and fast asleep I dared not try to wake lest this be just a dream and fast dissolve in glare of day/'cause dreams are sweet little things that come to tease you with the things you dare not do or cannot have/the things you fantasize about/would love to take into the upper air but cannot do and dare not make/lest real world squeals do break your bones as they turn you on the prejudicial wheels/but casting these dull thoughts aside which like cold showers before sun can render its hot beams the sweeter and more rich when rain has gone/now, came upon my ears some cracking twigs proclaiming this dream's not all mist/I scarcely breathed knew not if dream or bold reality stunned my brain/I cared not but still fastened lids and dreamy globes did rise and fall inside my inner universe oblivious to all except the sound which closer grew/I screwed all my attention to its source like radar scan and now the sound was caught inside my web was scrutinized inspected by taut nerves that stretched to catch the very air caught on the breath/and now sweet thin and piping words hung on my web like fireflies/mere traces/nothing clear but now I hear a sound like 'oh helen let's sit here'/helen! so I even knew the name of one/the intimate clue could call the sound and know its magic would resound inside her sweet ear and make her turn her face to where I lay/heart pounding like tarquin before lucrece's rape/

So down they sat while I in grass so tall did spy, and heard their giggling sounds add yet more music to the air so thick in warble chirp and wind that whistles through my secret lair/

they came to make love to the sun and shed their girly weeds
upon the bank/oh hot I was and thrilled to view this yet
delightful early morning dew/this unripe rose this unpicked
fruit/so just as if to catch the warm and rampant sunrays
'tween their thighs she paused, chin cupped in hands as if in
clouds of schoolgirls' dreamy thoughts/while down below the
bulging sun did play his golden fingers o'er her cunt/and my
eye did send a ray of light to snare in the sweet open air her
sight/of cupid sweetened and unblemished white/her shining
schoolgirl flag/which now with idle fingers underwaist she
scooped unpeeling like a second skin does from a snake/and
up she lifts her smooth curvaceous bum/two full moons rising
as the knickers slide down and one leg at a time is eased from
silky cotton fantasies of schoolboys' listless classroom
dreams/her small soft crest/her tender mouse was clinging on
between the marble columns of her house/and then behold
she lay down on the green and dewy bank/eyes closed against
the heavens' piercing eye/and then I saw her very flanks
unfold reveal the choice part of her thighs/they seemed to
glisten in the light fresh haze of summer's bee-droned endless
days between a slender tulip or, like a peapod opened fresh or
velvet petals of some flower all hungry for the sun's warm
shafts to ooze its yellow molten thru' its heart/it opens slowly
now to face the trickling hot rays from the sun's embrace/'oh
lovely now' she sighs and gurgles in falsetto rippling flute, 'if
only now . . .' and this I can't believe but heard the words
bruise past my ear/heard them detonate loud and clear with
. . . 'if only now I had a man's silk prick all would be fine/a
big and juicy horn to play with'/'hmmm' her friend agrees 'a
thick hard juicy prick to stick in here . . .' when even now the
thought draws one small tear to weep for joy between my thighs
and from my throat big lusty sighs/I pinched myself in dis-
belief is this a fantasy or wicked dream sent by the devil in
cunning jest that has you grasping out for snatch/your arms
around some luscious girl and then just as you're to drink your
fill awake rudely to mum in curls/but no, 'twas not a dream/
not even when like sirens' sighing on the wine-dark seas did
try to lure poor ulysses/they played and frolicked endlessly/

57

thrusting their fingers like five keen slaves ready to obey her every whim/they danced and played sweet lusty tunes upon her soft and aching quim/

'O fuck me,' one was saying now, 'o lovely man please fuck my lovely burning cunt/it's hot and runny dripping for a big thick slice of horny pan'/their eyes were closed tight in their trance so self-inflicted by sweet lust/the child not broken in or satisfied by hot young roughs/so sadly they must fantasize until some young pink prick gives them their fill/my tool by now was like a greyhound in the trap bursting to escape and pour its sap upon those open flowers/whose honey spilled so wastefully on the grass/so trembling I undid my bursting flies/I was all thumbs but out it sprung and reared its head/its knob all big and angry red, ready to spit its load and quench the fire down below/where those two sweet urchins did moan/so stealthily and not to fright I crawled through the long grass to where the sight and smell did draw my swelling beast and now half swooning in the summer's heat/I could almost reach out and touch their feet/the air stood still and hung so heavy in the perfumed auburn summer and late afternoon while shadows crawled like inky stains/I crept snakelike upon these maids who writhed like thrashing waves beneath a storm-lashed sky/imagine there I was, just framed in space on hands and knees/my cock a trumpet leading on or like the cannon loaded to heave its lead upon the enemy's head/then suddenly as if just on the crest of some great mountain peak/the child seemed to have reached/for now her face broke in a smile and shrieked out in her joy o god o god it's there/I heard the rapture in her voice make shock waves in the english teatime air/I thought 'tis now/just follow where your cock will thrive/go in and say hallo! it's good to be alive/ my penis swollen aching to be let loose/dragging me like some great stallion on its way to home will start to canter when it sniffs familiar roads/so now in twitches jumps and starts/ I'm ready, can't hold back, I'm home at last/the birds did stop eyes watch/even the wind, it seemed to drop/when suddenly in that split second beheld by thousands, insects, moles and birds. Each keen to see the rite performed that has gone on

58

since life on earth unfurled/when in that second/cock on fire/
a pearl worn on the blind eye of my love/or like my cock did
shed a tear in sheer relief to quench at last this biting thirsty
beast/so in that second held in time/all silent/golden warm
and air like wine/so just then/just in that split second/
thighs all tense like springs ready to pounce/so just then in
that same second she awoke and screamed 'oh fuck helen
here's a dirty bloke' .../her shrieks tore from the air the
fine embroidery/the great design that had with care been
sewn/each stitch to lead to the great masterpiece/the final act
not yet wove in/like the great masters saving for the end the
coup de grâce to relish all the more the sweetness of the central
core/the burning motive from which all else provides the
background score/so watched I now with grief the stitches
torn apart and dropped/the canvas smeared the story ripped
in two to be rewrote/and gazed in sadness as I watched the two
dissolve in dust shook up by rushing schoolgirl feet and
dumbly contemplated my puzzled and now shrinking meat/

The day was grey now clouds had stamped themselves
across the day with muddy hobnailed boots/but still thin
piercing beams did struggle and did spill some yellow paint
upon a lonely daffodil/I tramped home low in spirit and in
cock/the dream that came to life dissolved as if 'twas pierced
and stabbed with bloody knife/my head ablaze decided to
avenge the lust that raged within my groin/so off to local
sauna/high street cheam/the first time that I had to my local
been/I thought it wiser not to be seen by evil eyes/this town is
full of dreary spies that love to identify a figure's disappearing
back and then to say didn't I see you in the high street sauna
the other day/but now my caution's thrown about like some
great schooner on the rampant seas that seeks a harbour any-
where just for some peace/

MUM: Another day of blissful graft/have a nice day love/'twas
good to see the men of england going home all happy to their
tea/no more will infants feel the bloody kick/nor mother
nurse a blackened eye since jack and albert, jeff and fred will
be released in cock and head and be all peaceful, like before
the set [tv] and chortle at the football/go to bed/a quiet fart

under eiderdown, g'night love/up and down the breadth of royal england from noble prince to dustman bill/turn out the light luv echoes still, from voices all content with secret thrill from furtive hour with their local whore/I've had them all pop in their joints for basting/from blue blood cock all white and thin/stuttering as he tries to stick it in to giant darkie whose protuberance precedes his owner by five mins at least/we need then two rooms to receive the roll of flesh before it shrinks/so now home to my joe/but hush there is the bell/I suppose I can accommodate one last seminal spill:

DAD: I hope she's nice.

MUM: (Not recognizing him in the dark) Hallo, duckie you're just in time/not seen you before/oil or powder what's your choice/come sweetheart now where's your voice/you've gone a little shy/now that's ok/relax we'll make it go away/

DAD: (Aside) *Ye gods/I dare not look around but those words that emanate from out that gob sound like my old lady/oh ye gods/it can't be/shit and piss and throw in arseholes too/she sounds the same as maureen does/oh cruel fate to torment me like this/I am undone oh bollocks cocks and tits/*

MUM: (Dawning) *Hold on now, maureen, but that back with spotted bum like roses in a field of snow or raisins in some porridgey scum looks all familiar like old joe's/that voice was gruff and tired like joe once home from day of selfless graft he'd flop into armchair and burp all happy then to be indoors with glass of guinness and familiar moan/*

DAD: *Oh canker, oh rash of tosspots but that smell/those hands with soft and squishy squeeze seem by me to have been seen in other places like and shall I guess/washing up dishes in our old nest/oh cock and arsenal spurs as well/bobby charlton throw in the lot/I'd trade to get me out of this hell spot.*

MUM: *Oh fuck and sausages that turn to snakes oh blast of hell that now within my gut awakes the writhing serpent gnawing/now undone the trick has been found out/the tide of money that flowed with spunk/like ease has now washed back with acid bite and cobra's lash/*

DAD: *Oh god/let the floor open and swallow me/whole like jonah was by the mighty whale/and then spat out in some new place where*

she could never see my face / my shame inscribed my habit exposed
with trousers down / no teeming hard-on now but shrunken rose /

MUM: *Aye, 'tis true / my old man wandered in no doubt informed by*
some vile snooping lout some bastard perchance strolling in
informed him that I work in sin or so they call it / those that take
advantage / those that sneak off in a secret hour for subtle flick of
wrist or hire of flower that ignites those parts that other wives fail to
reach / they have informed on me / those dirty beasts /

DAD: *Hang on, before my shame and guilt take hold as doth a noose to*
hang me high / then what's my old lady doing looking spry in
panties frothed with lace and naked thighs / the dirty whore who
now for some time didst say goodnight with parting kiss / roll over
with a face all creased in bliss / so this is where the filthy whore did
dwell / my wife was milking cocks in this red-lighted stinking pit of
hell / oh farewell peace / oh farewell joy / my wife's dear precious
cunt was just for all the world a thing to use / their toy!

MUM: (Deciding to come clean) Hallo love / what you doing
here? / doth come to spy your wife I fear / some nasty turds
have spun some foul and horrid verbs inside your ear / all right
the game's up / I confess it's true / what next / divorce or
shame / so kick me out / you've caught me on the game /

DAD: (Aside) *Thank god she thinks I only came to spy / I did not know*
my trouble and strife / my darling wife was in the market of open
flies / but she believes in blameless quest / I came to discover this
hornets' nest / this darkened hell hole of the pumping wrist / and oh
my precious mary's mixed up in this / I'll be an actor . . . you filthy
slag! you dirty whore / I could not believe of those that told me
what goes on behind this door / my darling wife has flogged her
rose / my flower / my ornament of joy / my sceptre / my own doughnut
the furry cup that slaked my toy when it was thirsty dipping in and
stirring up all innocent the muck that's in this bin of sin / my little
mouse / my winking puss / that's probably seen the cocks of half the
town / that's tossed its sheckles into your greasy pockets / oh rage / oh
slimy mildewed canker / lukewarm tea / choirs on telly / pubs closed
at three / the rolling stones and vera lynn / oh curses high and foul on
thee / take thatcher powell even benn / I curse on thee that lot of
them /

MUM: Oh how your words do thrash like whips and cut my heart and soul to bits/my husband ne'er again will lay his head/all snoring in our precious bed/who needs the cash the filthy dough when in the end your karma knows and throws it back like hailstones hard and sharp/it tears the veil perfumed but thin/the stinking lard comes thru' and foul corruption too/ but know my sweet I did it for us both to line our future with some easy dough/but gave some comfort on the way/to those who at the end of slog in factory and pit have no sweet mate to take the ache and pain from it/

DAD: How foul you toad/you whore/who knows now oh god! maybe I'm carrying some obnoxious sore/that's slowly eating away poor me/

MUM: No sweet fear not/their weapons always were well sheathed/no never was abused I swear/and checked by doctor/everywhere who vouchsafed my purity and health/I would not don't you fear conceal by subterfuge deceit and stealth some canker that would eat away *your* health.

DAD: O god/o shatterer of souls/o blinding light/remove from me this awful sight/let me escape from seedy pit where snakes unroll their foul spit and suck down good old high street air which is like nectar or ambrosia compared to this unwholesome lair/

MUM: Forgive me, frank/give me a chance/I'll give up/never more to swing a leg or wrist to make pneumatic dance/the money, let it rot and stink/

DAD: (Aside) *Now hang about/let's not excite our wrath/we're out the storm, I'm safe in harbour/do not bite the hand that feeds/the horn of plenty she has tapped ... or squeezed/why throw it out/*
      (To her) So what's it all about?

MUM: What...?

DAD: I mean like I can understand.../you need a little more than I/can rustle up in weekly skive/

MUM: No, I will give it up/will never more I swear joe/I will work in woollies' [woolworths'] or elsewhere/if you will have me back/oh joe I'm on the rack/I'll scrub floors/anything to take the sting from being just a whore/

DAD: You make a bundle every week.

MUM: I make enough to make our future sweet/

DAD: You'll bring it home and split it you and me.

MUM: You mean to say...

DAD: (Emotionally) Why give up such lucrative pay?

MUM: Oh joe, you'll be a pimp!

DAD: Who cares/who wants to save and scrimp/now I'm getting over the first shock/I now admire/no talk of sin/free enterprise/there's gold in cock/we have to adjust now to the times/and morals are ok for those who can afford to be so wise/but us who get screwed every day/by boss then state who drains our pay/are not so bound to legal graft/when others thieve and rob/aye there's the rub for who would bear the whips when there's a fortune to be made in pricks/so doll I say I do forgive your ways/

MUM: Oh joe/I'm overcome with joy/we'll be a partnership you'll see/toys I'll buy that will delight all free from grubby tax collectors' greed/and when our fortune's made a house in sunny spain and swim and bake/

DAD: Sounds good to me/so love I do forgive and beg of thee/ since I am here and to tell true am slightly turned on by your gear/if you would donate free my dear/one of your samples for a treat/I'm feeling like a dog in heat/

MUM: Of course my love/it's been some time since you have wished a dip in mine/

DAD: Must be the atmosphere or role/for now I must confess/I find you rather *more* exotic now I see my wife's a whore/

MUM: Oh joe, you've made me proud/I'll give you what you ever dreamed/unleash your fantasies to me and I'll give you the best you'll see/describe the innermost dark secrets of your soul/your bestial cravings/anything goes!

DAD: Er ... I think I'll have relief today ... with topless too, if that's ok?

(Blackout.)